JA 03 '02	DATE DUE	
AP 09 '03		
AP 17 '03		

BIO MON

Selected from "Borrowed
Time"
Paul Monette
AR B.L.: 6.3
Points: 1.0

Selected from

BORROWED TIME
An AIDS Memoir

• ■ •

Paul Monette

Supplementary material by
Patricia Fogarty
and the staff of
Literacy Volunteers of New York City

WRITERS' VOICES
Literacy Volunteers of New York City

WRITERS' VOICES ™ was made possible by grants from: An anonymous foundation; The Vincent Astor Foundation; Exxon Corporation; Knight Foundation; Scripps Howard Foundation; Uris Brothers Foundation and H.W. Wilson Foundation.

ATTENTION READERS: We would like to hear what you think about our books. Please send your comments or suggestions to:

The Editors
Literacy Volunteers of New York City
121 Avenue of the Americas
New York, NY 10013

Selection: From BORROWED TIME: AN AIDS MEMOIR by Paul Monette. Copyright © 1988 by Paul Monette, reprinted by permission of Harcourt Brace Jovanovich, Inc.
Supplementary materials © 1992 by Literacy Volunteers of New York City Inc.

Printed in the United States of America.

98 97 96 95 94 93 92 10 9 8 7 6 5 4 3 2 1
First LVNYC Printing: May 1992
ISBN 0-929631-56-0

Writers' Voices is a series of books published by Literacy Volunteers of New York City Inc., 121 Avenue of the Americas, New York, NY 10013. The words, "Writers' Voices," are a trademark of Literacy Volunteers of New York City.

Cover designed by Paul Davis Studio.
Interior designed by Jules Perlmutter, Off-Broadway Graphics.

Publishing Director, LVNYC: Nancy McCord
Managing Editor: Sarah Kirshner
Publishing Coordinator: Yvette Martinez-Gonzalez
Marketing and Production Manager: Elizabeth Bluemle

LVNYC is an affiliate of Literacy Volunteers of America.

Acknowledgments

• ■ •

*L*iteracy Volunteers of New York City gratefully acknowledges the generous support of the following foundations and corporations that made the publication of WRITERS' VOICES and NEW WRITERS' VOICES possible: An anonymous foundation; The Vincent Astor Foundation; Exxon Corporation; Knight Foundation; Scripps Howard Foundation; Uris Brothers Foundation and H.W. Wilson Foundation.

This book could not have been realized without the kind and generous cooperation of the author, Paul Monette, and his publisher, Harcourt Brace Jovanovich, Inc. Thanks to Ellen Goulet, Permissions Department.

We deeply appreciate the contributions of the following suppliers: Cam Steel Rule Die Works Inc. (steel cutting die for display); Canadian Pacific Forest Products, Ltd. (text stock); Creative Graphics, Inc. (text typesetting); Westvāco Corporation (cover stock); MCUSA (display header); Delta Corrugated Container (corrugated display); Stevenson Photo Color Company (cover color separations); Coral Graphics Services, Inc. (cover printing); and R.R. Donnelly & Sons, Company (text printing and binding).

For their guidance, support and hard work, we are indebted to the LVNYC Board of Directors' Publishing Committee: James E. Galton, Marvel Comics Ltd.; Virginia Barber, Virginia Barber Literary Agency, Inc.; Doris Bass, Scholastic Inc.; Jeff Brown; Jerry Butler, William Morrow & Company, Inc.; George P. Davidson, Ballantine Books; Joy M. Gannon, St. Martin's Press; Walter Kiechel, *Fortune*; Geraldine E. Rhoads; Virginia Rice, Reader's Digest;

Martin Singerman, News America Publishing, Inc.; James L. Stanko, James Money Management, Inc. and F. Robert Stein, Pryor, Cashman, Sherman & Flynn.

Thanks also to George Davidson, Caron Harris and Steve Palmer of Ballantine Books for producing this book; Virginia Barber for help in obtaining permissions; Patricia Fogarty for her skill and diligence in the research and writing of the supplementary material for this book; Alison Mitchell for her thoughtful copyediting and suggestions; and to Pam Johnson for proofreading. Thanks to F. Robert Stein for legal advice and to Eli Zal for recommending this book.

Our thanks to Paul Davis Studio and Myrna Davis, Paul Davis, Lisa Mazur, Chalkley Calderwood and Alex Ginns for their inspired design of the covers of these books. Thanks also to Jules Perlmutter for his sensitive design of the interior of this book. Thanks also to AnneLouise Burns for design of maps and diagrams.

And finally, special credit must be given to Marilyn Boutwell, Jean Fargo and Gary Murphy of the LVNYC staff for their contributions to the educational and editorial content of these books.

Contents

· ■ ·

Note to the Reader

• ■ •

Borrowed Time: An AIDS Memoir is the true story of how Roger Horwitz became sick with AIDS and eventually died of its effects. The book was written by Paul Monette, who had been Roger's longtime companion when Roger became sick. The book begins after Roger has died and Paul himself has the AIDS virus. The main story of the book is Paul's memories of Roger's illness. These memories begin with the time before Roger's illness was diagnosed and continue until Roger's death.

Every writer has a special voice. That is why we call our series *Writers' Voices*. We chose *Borrowed Time* because Paul Monette's voice can be clearly heard as he describes the pain and sadness, the anger and fear that he and Roger lived through. But the book is also a moving record of the love the two men shared.

Our selection is from the first part of *Borrowed Time*. After Roger has died, Paul looks back in time to the beginning of Roger's illness, when very few people had heard of AIDS. Our selection includes Paul's memories of the events that took place up until the day doctors told the two men that Roger had AIDS.

Our book has several different chapters in addition to the selection itself. They provide background information that can help you in understanding the selection. You may choose to read some or all of these chapters before or after reading the selection.

- Reading "About the Selection from *Borrowed Time: An AIDS Memoir*" on page 10 will help you to begin thinking about the characters and the setting of the story.

- If you would like more information about AIDS, look at the chapters called "An Update on AIDS" on page 51, and "Where to Get More Information about AIDS and Treatment Options" on page 58. They contain questions and answers about AIDS, as well as telephone numbers to call for further information and testing and treatment programs.

- Many readers enjoy finding out about the person who wrote a selection. Sometimes this information will give you more insight into the selection. You can learn more about Paul Monette in the chapter on page 49.

If you are a new reader, you may want to have this book read aloud to you, perhaps more than once. Even if you are a more experienced reader, you may enjoy hearing it read aloud before reading it silently to yourself.

We encourage you to read *actively*. Here are some things you can do.

Before Reading

- Read the front and back covers of the book, and look at the cover illustration. Ask yourself what you expect the book to be about.

- Think about why you want to read this book. Perhaps you want to find out more about AIDS. Perhaps you know someone who has AIDS.

- Look at the Contents page. See where you can find a chronology of events in the selection as they relate to the history of AIDS and other information. Decide what you want to read and in what order.

During Reading

- There may be medical terms or other words that are difficult to read. Keep reading to see if the meaning becomes clear. If it doesn't, ask someone for the word. Or look up the words in the dictionary. The medical terms in **bold** type in the text are defined in the glossary on page 61.

- Ask yourself questions as you read. For example: How would you react if someone you loved was threatened by an incurable disease?

After Reading

- Think about what you have read. Did you identify with the writer? Did the selection give you any new information? Did it help you think about issues related to AIDS?
- Talk with others about your thoughts.
- Try some of the questions and activities in "Questions for the Reader" on page 45. They are meant to help you discover more about what you have read and how it relates to you.

The editors of *Writers' Voices* hope you will write to us. We want to know your thoughts about our books.

About the Selection from *Borrowed Time: An AIDS Memoir*

• ■ •

*I*n 1974 Paul Monette, a writer, and Roger Horwitz, a lawyer, met in Boston, Massachusetts, where they fell in love and started living together. In 1977 they moved to Los Angeles, California, where Monette wrote poetry, novels and screenplays, and Horwitz practiced law.

Borrowed Time: An AIDS Memoir is about the relationship of these two men. In the early 1980s they began to learn about AIDS (Acquired Immune Deficiency Syndrome), a mysterious disease which, at that time, mainly afflicted gay men. The selection focuses on the ways Monette and Horwitz responded to the threat and finally to the reality of an incurable disease. In this selection from *Borrowed Time*, other characters also appear, such as Roger's parents and Dr. Dennis Cope, Roger's doctor at the University of California at Los Angeles (UCLA) hospital.

Monette and Horwitz learned about friends coming down with AIDS and about the growing numbers of sick people in New York and San Francisco. Their fear grew, along with their frustration, for very little was known about AIDS in the early 1980s.

In the early 1980s no one knew exactly how AIDS passed from person to person. People only knew they had it when they got very sick. People were passing it to one another without knowing it. Many men in the gay community had gotten the AIDS virus but didn't know they had it or how they got it. The threat of the mysterious sickness made people feel helpless and frightened. Monette compares it to a war, to facing a battle without weapons to fight back.

What kept Monette and Horwitz going was their love for one another. They had always had a strong bond, but they became even closer as their worst fears came true. After they found out that Horwitz had AIDS, their love sustained them and gave them strength.

The selection from *Borrowed Time* contains some medical terms. The medical terms in **bold** type are defined in the glossary on page 61.

The chronology on page 14 shows the events described in the selection as they relate to the history of AIDS. Roger Horwitz was one of the first people to take AZT, a new antiviral drugs that helps block the growth of the AIDS virus within the body.

Since Roger Horwitz died, scientists have learned more about the AIDS virus, which is called HIV (Human Immunodeficiency Virus). There have been some hopeful medical advances in the treatment of HIV and the symptoms of AIDS. People are living longer after being infected with the virus. But still no cure has been found. (See "An Update on AIDS," on page 51.)

As of December 1991, nearly 203,000 people in the United States had been diagnosed with AIDS since 1981. About 58% were homosexual or bisexual, about 28% were intravenous drug users, and about 6% were heterosexual. Women account for 10% of the cases of AIDS. Of the total cases of AIDS, 54% were white, 29% black, and 16% Hispanic. More than 64% (over 130,000) of the people who have been diagnosed with AIDS have died. It has been estimated that at least one million people in the United States carry the HIV virus. The HIV virus is spreading in the heterosexual population in the United States. In November 1991, basketball star Magic Johnson announced he had the virus.

The subtitle of *Borrowed Time* is *An AIDS Memoir*. "Memoir" comes from a French word that means "memory." Paul Monette's highly personal writing style makes the selection from *Borrowed Time* a vivid replay of his painful memories of Roger Horwitz's sickness and death. The reader can feel Monette's fear and anger, his frustration and terrible sadness, and, above all, his great love for his friend.

Perhaps the selection will remind you of a time when you or someone you loved was very ill. Perhaps it will make you think about how love can keep people going even in the face of death.

Chronology of Events

• ■ •

Dates in the History of AIDS

Summer 1981	The first four cases of AIDS are reported.
July 1983	The virus that causes AIDS is discovered.
March 1985	More than 9,000 people, mostly gay men, have been diagnosed with AIDS.
March 1985	The test for antibodies to the HIV virus is introduced (see "An Update on AIDS," page 51).
April 1985	The first international AIDS conference is held in Atlanta, Georgia.
1986	Doctors begin to prescribe antiviral drugs to block the HIV virus.

Dates in the Selection from
Borrowed Time: An AIDS Memoir

September 1974	Paul Monette and Roger Horwitz meet and fall in love.
October 1981	Horwitz has a bad case of "flu."
February 1982	Monette and Horwitz begin to take safe-sex precautions.
February 1985	Horwitz again comes down with what he thinks is the flu.
March 12, 1985	Horwitz is diagnosed with AIDS.
October 22, 1986	Roger Horwitz dies.
1988	*Borrowed Time: An AIDS Memoir* is published.

Map of Places Mentioned
in the Selection

♦

Boston
MASSACHUSETTS

New York City
NEW YORK

San Francisco
CALIFORNIA

Los Angeles
CALIFORNIA

United States of America

Selected from

BORROWED TIME
An AIDS Memoir

• ■ •

Paul Monette

I don't know if I will live to finish this. Maybe it's just that I've watched too many sicken in a month and die by Christmas, so that a fatal sort of realism comforts me more than magic. All I know is this: The virus ticks in me. No one has solved the puzzle of its timing. I take my drug from Tijuana twice a day. The very friends who tell me how vigorous I look, how well I seem, are the first to assure me of the imminent medical break-through. What they don't seem to understand is, I used up all my optimism keeping my friend alive. Now that he's gone, the cup of my own health is neither half full nor half empty. Just half.

Equally difficult, of course, is knowing where to start. The world around me is defined now by its endings and its closures—the date on the grave that follows the hyphen. Roger Horwitz, my beloved friend, died of complications of AIDS on October 22, 1986, nineteen months and ten days after his diagnosis. That is the only real date anymore, casting its ice shadow over all the secular holidays lovers mark their calendars by. Until that long night in October, it didn't seem possible that any day could supplant the brute equinox of March 12—the day of Roger's diagnosis in 1985, the day we began to live on the moon.

The fact is, no one knows where to start with AIDS. Now, in the seventh year of the calamity, my friends in L.A. can hardly recall what it felt like any longer, the time before the sickness. Yet we all watched the toll mount in New York, then in San Francisco, for years before it ever touched us here. It comes like a slowly dawning horror. At first you are equipped with a hundred different amulets to keep it far away. Then someone you know goes into the hospital, and suddenly you are at high noon in full battle gear. They have neglected to tell you that you will be issued no weapons of any sort. So you cobble together a weapon out of anything that lies at hand, like a prisoner honing a spoon handle into a stiletto. You fight tough, you fight dirty, but you cannot fight dirtier than it.

I remember a Saturday in February 1982, driving Route 10 to Palm Springs with Roger to visit his parents for the weekend. While Roger drove, I read aloud an article from **The Advocate**: "Is Sex Making Us Sick?" The article didn't mince words. It was the first in-depth reporting I'd read that laid out the shadowy nonfacts of what till then had been the most fragmented of rumors. The first cases were reported to the Centers for Disease Control (CDC) only six months before, but they weren't in the newspapers, not in L.A.

I remember exactly what was going through my mind while I was reading, though I can't now recall the details of the piece. I was thinking: How is this not me? Trying to find a pattern I was exempt from. It was a brand of denial I would watch grow exponentially during the next few years, but at the time I was simply relieved.

Not us.

I grabbed for that relief because we'd been through a rough patch the previous autumn. Till then Roger had always enjoyed a sort of no-nonsense good health. In the seven years we'd been together I scarcely remember him having a cold or taking an aspirin. Yet in October '81 he had struggled with a peculiar bout of **intestinal flu**. Nothing special showed up in any of the blood tests, but over a period of weeks he experienced persistent symptoms that didn't neatly connect: pains in his legs, diarrhea, general malaise. I hadn't been feeling notably bad myself, but on the other hand I was a textbook hypochondriac, and I figured if Rog was harboring some kind of bug, so was I.

The tests came back positive for **amoebiasis**. Roger and I began the highly toxic treatment to kill the amoeba, involving two separate drugs and what seems in memory thirty pills a day for six weeks, till the middle of January. It was the first time I'd ever experienced the phenomenon of the cure making you sicker. By the end of treatment we were both weak and had lost weight, and for a couple of months afterward were susceptible to colds and minor infections.

So it wasn't the *Advocate* story that sent up the red flag for us. We'd been shaken by the amoeba business, and from that point on we operated at a new level of sexual caution. What is now called safe sex did not use to be so clearly defined. The concept didn't exist. But it was quickly becoming apparent, even then, that we couldn't wait for somebody else to define the parameters. Thus every gay man I know has had to come to a point of personal definition by way of avoiding the chaos of sexually transmitted diseases, or STD as we call them in the trade. The party was going to have to stop. The evidence was too ominous: *We were making ourselves sick.*

Not that Roger and I were the life of the party. In ten years he [Roger] had perhaps half a dozen contacts outside the main frame of our relationship, mostly when he was out of town on business. He was comfortable with relative monogamy. I was the one in the relationship who suffered from lost time. I was the one who would go after a sexual encounter as if it were an ice cream cone—casual, quick, good-bye.

I only want to make it plain to start with that we got very alert and very careful as far back as the winter of '82. That gut need for safety took hold and lingered, even as we got better again and strong. Thus I'm not entirely sure what I thought on another afternoon a year and a half later, when a friend of ours back from New York reported a conversation he'd had with a research man from Sloan-Kettering [a cancer center].

"He thinks all it takes is one exposure," Charlie said, this after months of articles about the significance of repeated exposure. More tenaciously than ever, we all wanted to believe the whole deepening tragedy was centered on those at the sexual frontiers who were fucking their brains out.

Yet with caution as our watchword starting in February of '82, Roger was diagnosed with AIDS three years later. So the turning over of new leaves was not to be on everybody's side. A lot of us were already ticking and didn't even know.

How do I speak of the person who was my life's best reason? The most completely unpretentious man I ever met, modest and decent to such a degree that he seemed to release what was most real in everyone he knew. It was always a relief to be with Roger, not to have to play any games at all.

He had a contagious, impish sense of humor, especially about the folly of things, especially self-importance. Yet he was blissfully unfrivolous, without a clue as to what was "in." He had thought life through somehow and come out the other side with a proper respect for small pleasures. Roger loved nothing better than a one-on-one talk with a friend, and he had never lost track of a single one, all the way back to high school. The luck of the draw was mine, for I was the best and the most.

We met on the eve of Labor Day in 1974, at a dinner party at a mutual friend's apartment on Beacon Hill, just two days before Roger was to start work as an attorney at a stately firm in Boston. He was thirty-two; I was twenty-eight. Summer has always been good to me, even the bittersweet end, with the slant of yellow light, and I for one was in love before the night was done. I suppose we'd been waiting for each other all our lives. The business of coming out had been difficult for both of us, partly because of the closet nature of all relations in a Puritan town like Boston, partly because we were both so sure of what we wanted and it kept not coming to life.

For if there was no man out there who was equal and **simpatico**, then what was the point of being gay? The baggage and the shit you had to take were bad enough. But it all jogged into place when we met. My life was a sort of amnesia till then, longing for something that couldn't be true until I'd found the rest of me. Is that feeling so different in straight people? Or is it that gay people have to keep it secret and so grow divided, with a bachelor's face to the world and a pang like dying inside?

We weren't kids anymore. We'd been hurting dull as a toothache for years. When we came together as lovers we knew precisely how happy we were. I only realized then that I'd never had someone to play with before. Six weeks before Roger died, he looked over at me astonished one day in the hospital, eyes dim with the gathering blindness. "But we're the same person," he said in a sort of bewildered delight. "When did that happen?"

· ■ ·

I always hesitate over the marriage word. It's inexact and exactly right at the same time, but of course I don't have a legal leg to stand on. The deed to the house on Kings Road says *a single man* after each of our names. So much for the lies of the law. There used to be gay marriages in the ancient world, even in the early Christian church. And yet I never felt quite comfortable calling Rog my lover. To me it smacked too much of the ephemeral, with a beaded sixties topspin. *Friend* always seemed more intimate to me, more flush with feeling. Ten years after we met, there would still be occasions when we'd find ourselves among strangers of the straight persuasion, and one of us would say, "This is my friend." It never failed to quicken my heart, to say it or overhear it. *Little friend* was the diminutive form we used in private, the phrase that is fired in bronze beneath his name on the hill.

· ■ ·

Over and over I've watched those who are stricken fight their way back to some measure of health and go on working—those who are not let go, that is. Perhaps the work is especially important because AIDS is striking so many of us just as we're hitting our stride at work. I mean of course the American AIDS of the first half-decade, before it began to burgeon in the black and brown communities. Most of the fallen in our years were urban gay men, and most of these were hard at their work when the symptoms started multiplying and nothing would go away. They wanted to hold on to their work as long as they could.

Roger was no different, and neither am I. With him gone, there is just what work I can finish before it overtakes me. Again there are friends all around me, meaning well, who say I don't have to feel so cornered: New treatments are coming down the pipeline every day; the **antivirals** data looks better and better. Et cetera. Perhaps it is just very human to want to die with your boots on. I don't know if that's a cowboy or a combat metaphor, but both are perfectly apt.

After six years in the house on Kings Road, we'd fallen into a pattern of optimum tranquillity. Our most consistent time together—though we'd pick up the phone all day and call—was evenings seven to eleven. Some tag end of the workday might spill over here and there, but we usually ate at home on weeknights, did some reading and went for a walk. My whole life is like one of those weeknights now, plain and quiet and, here in the house at least, close to Rog. A stucco thirties cottage high in a box canyon above the Sunset Strip. There's a view of the city lights through the coral tree out front and between the olive and the eucalyptus across the way.

There was always a sort of double clock to the evening, because Roger was asleep by midnight, never a night's insomnia, and I didn't go to bed till three. I typed like a dervish once the phone couldn't possibly ring. But I'd usually loll in bed with Rog for a half hour—Ted Koppel too, if the issue was ripe—and he'd nod off curled beside me, the two of us nestled like a pair of spoons. By way of trade-off I'd be half aware of him getting up at seven-thirty, padding about while I burrowed in for the morning, to rise at eleven. Between us we covered the night and the morning watch.

I realize now how peaceful it was to be writing while Rog lay asleep in the next room. I can't describe how safe it made me feel, how free to work. I think mothers must feel safe like that, when it's so late at night you can hear a baby breathe. We had gone along this way for so many years that when I had to do it for real—watch over him half the night, wake him and give him pills, run the **IV**, change his sweat-soaked pajamas three different times—it never stopped feeling safe, not when I had him at home. In the deep ultramarine of the night, nothing could really go wrong, and nothing ever did.

In 1984 increasing numbers of gay men are being diagnosed with AIDS. Although he has none of the symptoms, Monette lives in fear of the disease.

I knew all the warning signals now. Night sweats, fevers, weight loss, diarrhea, tongue sores, bruises that didn't heal. None of the above. But I'd run through them every day.

Any change, any slight modification . . . even a bruise you remembered the impact of, you'd watch like an x-ray till it started turning yellow around the purple. **KS** lesions do not go yellow. They also do not go white if you press them hard with your thumb. A whole gibberish of phrases and clues was beginning to gain currency. A canker sore in the mouth would ruin a day, for fear it was **thrush**—patches of white on the gums or the tongue. I read my tongue like a palmist before I went to bed at night.

In none of this paranoid fantasy did I have the slightest worry that Roger was at risk. I hadn't forgotten the flu in '81. There were shakes and fevers that winter, and for a week or two Roger would break out at night in hives the size of silver dollars. It had been an awful siege, but that was all three years ago now. Never a complainer about his health, he didn't mention losing weight till the end of November, and even then it was only a couple of pounds. He was tired at night, but a wholesome kind of tired, with a long untroubled slumber from twelve to seven-thirty like clockwork. And his cough was still such a minor two-note matter. He'd be putting on his pajamas, and I'd turn from *Nightline* and tease him: "What are you coughing for? Stop it." That was how ordinary it sounded.

Is that denial? If it was, it was warring in me with a doomed acceptance, as I struggled to figure how I would bear the sentence myself. Late at night I'd walk in the canyon and think about Roger watching me suffer. I was already riddled with guilt: None of this would be happening if I'd never had sex with strangers. I suppose I felt there was something innately shameful about dying of a **venereal disease**. All the self-hating years in the closet were not so far behind me.

· ◼ ·

Monette thinks back to a few years before when he and Roger told their families about being gay.

In '77 Roger and I had been living together in Boston for two years, and my parents had welcomed him into the family with pretty open arms. But nobody ever said the word *gay*. My own point of no return occurred when my first novel was about to be published. I slipped a copy of the bound galleys to my parents, figuring they'd better know what was coming before the book hit the stores. They reacted predictably, I suppose—telling me they would have to sell their house and leave town, that I'd never hold a job again with this infamy to my name, and besides, my mother had the idea I wasn't really gay. Roger was just a phase, I guess.

It's just an unavoidable mess, this coming-out business, and there don't appear to be any shortcuts through the emotions, though we try to make it easier for those who come after. Someday the process will be more human, perhaps, because we are open forever now, and people can't hate their children or themselves for that long.

When Roger finally sat his father down to tell him he was gay, we had been living together for six years, so obviously happy that to everyone around us we were a hyphenate, Roger-and-Paul, such a unified field had we become. [But] for the next year and a half Al [Roger's father] couldn't look me in the face, couldn't speak my name or enter our house. We got through it and were all very close now, as close as Roger had come to be to my family, but that doesn't mean that getting there was fun.

*In February 1985, Roger again comes down with what
he thinks is the flu.*

Next day he came home early from the office
and went to bed. It was then I told him he really
had to call Dr. Cope at UCLA. Not to panic, I
quickly added as he winced apprehensively, but he
could be harboring some sort of low-grade
walking pneumonia that needed antibiotics.
He agreed with a certain relief, comforted just to
be talking about it as a concrete thing with
beginning and end.

I cooked stevedore meals and pampered Rog all
weekend. "Everyone's got the flu, it's all over the
place, everyone says," I wrote two weeks later,
grasping at the straws of the flu tautology.

My journal gets very spotty here, with only a
single detailed entry for the whole sea change of
the next six weeks. I know the refrain of the next
month, from every side, was constant: *It's not, it
can't be.* Roger was the last man anyone thought
would get it.

My memory of those weeks, back and forth to
UCLA, is mostly shell-shock fragments. I can't
even put them in chronological order, let alone
weigh them. I know Roger spent three days in

bed, then tried one at the office, only to wilt and crash with another fever. That would be February 19, the day the water pipe burst in the bathroom off the guest room and another burst on Detroit Street, so we had plumbers slogging in and out, distracting us with the chaos of banality. Thursday Roger put in a full day at work, came home with [a fever of] 101.6 and logged yet another weekend in bed. He would seem to get stronger if he laid low for a day or two—he wasn't getting worse, just not getting better. People would drop by to visit, full of statistics about the alphabet of influenza coursing through the city like an ill wind from the East. How much denial was everyone practicing?

I was also running out of friends who weren't sick. Now I began to hyperventilate with panic and claustrophobia, the stakes seeming to double every time the phone rang. What morning was it that I first woke up suspended in that instant before a car wreck? The hysteria first to last was much more acute in me than in Roger. It's with a certain awe I look back and see how balanced and focused he stayed, even as he gathered and husbanded his strength, patiently trying to get back to work. It's not just that he wasn't a complainer, or that his attitude was stoic. That would come. It was rather that he took refuge now in his temperate nature, a capacity for quietness that began as instinct and ended as character.

More to the point, if Roger had great patience, I have none. Here at the pitch of emergency I can only lay out the fragments of what seared my frantic heart. I am the weather, Roger is the climate, and they are not always the same. Yet the careening of those next few weeks, fitting in visits to UCLA, more and more in tandem, is the story of a kind of bond that the growing oral history of AIDS records again and again. Whatever happened to Roger happened to me, and my numb strength was a crutch for all his frailty. It didn't feel like strength to me, or it was strength without qualities, pure raw force. Yet it took up the slack for Rog, and we somehow always got where we needed to be. In a way, I am only saying that I loved him—better than myself, no question of it—but increasingly every day that love became the only untouched shade in the dawning fireball.

Roger's blood was drawn fifteen different ways, but we had no test for **antibodies** yet, so none of

the numbers led anywhere. Still there was no
perceptible cough, and the general malaise and
zigzag fever weren't in themselves conclusive,
could still be that phantom flu, shimmering now
like an oasis.

On March 1 he [Dr. Cope] told us the chest
x-ray looked clear, except for a shadow that was
probably the **pulmonary artery**, but he was
playing safe and ordering a **CAT scan** to make
sure it wasn't a **lymph node**. Roger and I had
lunch that day at the hospital cafeteria, in the
prison-yard court on plastic chairs under a
lowering sky. Roger said how glad he was I was
there. My sentiments exactly: as long as we stood
our ground together we could thread our way
through this maze a step at a time, Buddha's way
to the top of the mountain.

A few days later when Roger went in to see
Cope, I ran out to the corridor and called a
friend, to grill him as to his own bout with
"regular" pneumonia the previous winter. There
had been a suspended day or two back then, as
we all waited uncomfortably for the man's results,
and then the tests proved negative for AIDS, and
we all went back to life. Now I gripped the phone
white-knuckled, hammering symptoms out of him.

One by one I compared them to Rog, pinning my case on that regular brand of infection. When I strode back to the waiting room, Roger was sitting there stunned, and he stumbled out into the hall as if my five minutes away had nearly let him drown. He sagged beside the water fountain and spoke in a kind of bewildered shock: "He says it could be **TB**."

Then he started to cry, and the burst of tears sent one of his contact lenses awry. So instead of holding him I had to cup my hands under his eye while he worked the lens back in, swallowing the scald of tears. That specific helpless moment, the soft disk swimming out onto his cheek, stuck with me like a pivot of agony. A year and a half later I'd still be trying to explain to Rog, when the talk came round to the horror, how in that noon moment I died inside. As if I would not live in a world where my friend could be in pain like this. I don't remember what happened then, if we had another test or were given leave to go home, but something had cracked that would never knit again.

A couple of days afterward we were eating a glazed breakfast before going off to UCLA. As I cleared the table—things in order if not life—Roger looked up at me and said: "It's just the two of us."

"I know," I replied, though of course we weren't alone.

All the same, it was just the two of us lining up as the tests grew more harrowing, the corridors at UCLA more like a separate equal world every day. Forgive us the feeling now and then that the woods had closed behind us. In the most visceral way, with a taste like a ball of blood in our mouths, it seemed that life itself was pulling in like a tortoise. Just us.

I was taking Roger's temperature every couple of hours now, shaking down the thermometer till I had a twinge like tennis elbow. One crazed afternoon I accidentally broke the thermometer against a door and fell to my knees keening, trying to pick up the shards as the mercury beaded into the jade-green carpet.

The **blood-gas** results proved to be in the normal range, which was a relief, yet there was clearly some kind of infection in the lung. The issue at week's end was whether or not that infection was "interstitial." **Pneumocystis carinii**—the deadly AIDS pneumonia, so-called PCP—is an interstitial infection, which means it invades the interstices between the lung sacs. A battery of x-rays seemed to indicate no interstitial involvement, and this was taken to be good news, especially by our doctor friends. We were pinning them down for opinions in matters that weren't their field, but they were generous here as they would be throughout. Once I heard the interstices were clear, I tossed the pneumocystis file away.

Despite the positive sign on the interstitial front, Roger still wasn't getting any better. Still not worse, but Cope decided it would only be prudent to have Roger come in for a **bronchoscopy**, in which a flexible tube is inserted in the lung for a specimen of tissue. The bronc has become such a fact of all our lives now, it's hard to recall there was a time I'd never heard of it.

Roger would have to go into the hospital overnight to have it. Neither of us had spent so much as a day in that nether place, not in our whole ten years together.

Over the weekend before he went in, we just hunkered down.

Roger was comfortable resting in bed, still no cough to speak of, animated with everyone who visited. Saturday night he convinced me to go out for dinner [with friends. Roger stayed home.]

When I got home, however, I found Rog sitting in the study coughing, and looking more drained, worn out and lost than he had all month. He was so glad to see me and be taken care of. At such a moment you move like an avalanche to oblige, for all the reasons of love but also just to keep busy. It was going to be fine, he'd be home by Tuesday afternoon, and after that there were no more tests. Then he would have to get better, I thought, as I kneaded his shoulders and curled him to sleep.

Al and Bernice [Roger's parents] had decided to drive in from the desert, even though we told them it wasn't necessary. They agreed to hold off till Monday and just stay overnight till we got the results of the bronc. On Sunday evening I fixed the two of us as cheery a supper as I could muster. Roger's appetite hadn't suffered, at least. But in the middle of the meal he excused himself to go to the bathroom, where he had a twinge of diarrhea. This didn't prove to lead to anything ominous on its own, and in fact through all his sickness Roger didn't have to deal with much intestinal static. But as I sat at the dining room table waiting for him to come back, the food like ashes on my tongue, I had a sudden vision of what a flimsy wall we'd been building the last few weeks, brick by brick.

He seemed so weak and overwhelmed by then, and the hardest thing to watch him lose in the early days was the spring in his step. He'd always had a quickness about him, a vigorous enthusiasm that I can still see in picture after picture out of the past, like a great store of potential energy. The wellspring of it wasn't athletic; it flowed from a joy of life. In the steepening decline of the previous months he'd lost the physical edge of that delight—lost it for good. Though he had reservoirs of deeper and sweeter tones to compensate, I missed the boyish energy most. Perhaps because mine went with it.

On the way to UCLA on Monday morning, driving along Sunset to the west side, Roger asked quietly: "What if it's really serious?"

Despite the positive talk all week—all month—and despite the fact that my last nickel was riding on denial. I don't know if I answered the right question, but I know my voice was steadier than I would've thought possible. Rog, I said, you have to understand how much everyone loves you.

I can't really separate the March 11 check-in on the tenth floor of the medical center from a dozen others. Amateurs still at the system, I expect we appeared like two meek refugees, with the overnight bag and a briefcase full of work. The tenth floor at UCLA is called the Wilson Pavilion, all private rooms and food prepared to order, the carpeted veneer of a hotel corridor not quite masking the naked high-tech sick gear.

We would both grow grimly accustomed to the first day of a hospitalization, with the interns sweeping in as if by revolving door, trying to look serious in spite of their comical youth, mad with backed-up things to do and racing like the White Rabbit. There would come a time when I would take over this phase, give the tedious history, answer the bald questions: Are you a homosexual? Are you or have you ever been an IV drug abuser? On March 11 I couldn't tell one intern from the next, intern from resident. I didn't realize that in a teaching hospital like UCLA every patient is one more unit to cover as they cram for the test of their budding careers. And here in the presence of a new disease, each kid doctor wanted an A. But remember, Roger was only supposed to be there overnight, so I held them all at arm's length and resisted differentiating.

Roger bore the process very well, and we seemed to be taking a proper stand of firmness in saying he was feeling not too bad. *Not sick enough, not sick enough*—I kept repeating Cope's phrase. It was still so, wasn't it? The pulmonary man came in to explain how the bronchoscopy worked. They would do it early in the morning, and we should probably have the results by noon. Home for lunch.

Dennis Cope was a welcome sight late in the day, because he at least knew who we were, and more to the point, the interns knew who he was.

I must've gone out for dinner with Al and Bernice, and I must've been full of reassurance and interstitial data. All the blood work was normal so far, but I don't recall if an actual **T-cell test** was taken, or if we knew the results before the verdict. The T cells are a subset of the white blood count. Infection with the AIDS virus reverses the T-cell ratio, indicating an **immune dysfunction**. A test was available at that time, but it was still considered exotic and far down the line of inquiry. Today I know fifteen people who have their T cells tested every six or eight weeks.

I also wonder now, in a sort of stupor, how it was we had no plan whatsoever if the news was bad. We hadn't ever discussed who would know and who wouldn't, how we would euphemize, indeed if hiding was even feasible. In a way it was like the whole last year, when we never talked about dying because we were fighting so hard to stay alive. I understand that in theory it's good to have these matters out, to make one's lifeboat plans and release the sum of one's worldly goods. But we didn't seem able to do that and forge ahead at the same time. Warriors in pitched battle do not make their last will; they become it.

I was over at UCLA on Tuesday morning before the pulmonary team, and his parents and I gave Roger a bracing squeeze. I stayed with him till the doctor came in to administer the local anesthetic, and then I waited in the empty lounge with Al and Bernice, watching them as they dutifully read their books, refusing to leave my watch when the two of them went for coffee.

Altogether it took maybe twenty minutes. I was in Roger's room the second the team walked out. Roger was lying on his side, with an oxygen mask over his nose and mouth. They'd told us he would need it till the anesthetic wore off. What they hadn't said was that he would be coughing, almost without stopping and clearly in real discomfort. I patted him and talked a bit, but we really couldn't communicate. Even if this was a predictable reaction to the procedure and nothing more, the reality was jarring in the extreme. For this was the very cough we'd always said wasn't there. Could things have changed so fast? And who among my advisers would have me not worry now?

Finally, the oxygen mask came off. Roger was so debilitated from the trauma of the test that he lay back in an exhausted sleep. I don't know how much time went by. When the doctors came in—a pair of them, the intern and the pulmonary man—they stayed as close to each other as they could, like puppies. They stood at his bedside, for the new enlightenment demands that a doctor not deliver doom from the foot of the bed, looming like God. The intern spoke: "Mr. Horwitz, we have the results of the bronchoscopy. It does show evidence of **pneumocystis** in the lungs."

Was there a pause for the world to stop? There must have been, because I remember the crack of silence, Roger staring at the two men. Then he simply shut his eyes, and only I, who was the rest of him, could see how stricken was the stillness in his face.

"We'll begin treatment immediately with **Bactrim**. You'll need to be here in the hospital for fourteen to twenty-one days. Do you have any questions?"

Roger shook his head on the pillow. I wanted to kill these two ridiculous young men with the nerdy plastic pen shields in their white-coat pockets. "Could you please leave us alone," I said.

And they tweedled out, relieved to have it over with. I ran around the bed and clutched Roger's hand. "We'll fight it, darling, we'll beat it, I promise. I won't let you die." The sentiments merged as they tumbled out. This is the liturgy of bonding. Mostly we clung together, as if time still had the decency to stop when we were entwined. After all, the whole world was right here in this room. I don't think Roger said anything then. Neither of us cried. It begins in a country beyond tears. Once you have your arms around your friend with his terrible news, your eyes are too shut to cry.

The intern had never once said the word.

· ■ ·

Questions
for the Reader

• ■ •

Thinking about the Story

1. What was interesting for you about the selection from *Borrowed Time: An AIDS Memoir?*

2. Did the events or people in the selection became important or special to you in some way? Write about or discuss your answers.

3. In what ways did the selection answer the questions you had before you began reading or listening?

4. Were any parts of the selection difficult to understand? If so, you may want to read or listen to them again. Discuss with your learning partners possible reasons why they were difficult.

Thinking about the Writing

1. How did Paul Monette help you see, hear and feel what happened to him and to Roger in the

selection? Find the words, phrases or sentences that did this best.

2. Writers of memoirs think carefully about what they will include in this very personal form of writing. What do you think Paul Monette felt was most important in writing this selection? Find the parts of the selection that support your opinion.

3. In the selection, Paul Monette recreates the fear and distress he felt in the face of AIDS. Go back to the story and find the parts that make you understand his fearful emotions.

4. In the selection from *Borrowed Time*, Paul Monette uses very little dialogue. Think about the effect that is created by this sparing use of dialogue.

Activities

1. Were there any words that were difficult for you in the selection from *Borrowed Time*? Go back to these words and try to figure out their meanings. Discuss what you think each word means, and why you made that guess. Look them up in a dictionary and see if your definitions are the same or different.

Discuss with your learning partners how you are going to remember each word. Some ways to remember words are to put them on file cards, write them in a journal or create a personal dictionary. Be sure to use the words in your writing in a way that will help you to remember their meanings.

2. Talking with other people about what you have read can increase your understanding. Discussion can help you organize your thoughts, get new ideas and rethink your original ideas. Discuss your thoughts about the selection from *Borrowed Time* with someone else who has read it. Find out if you helped yourselves understand the selection in the same or different ways. Find out if your opinions about the selection are the same or different. See if your thoughts change as a result of this discussion.

3. After you finish reading or listening, you might want to write down your thoughts about the book. You could write your reflections on the book in a journal, or you could write about topics the book has brought up that you want to explore further. You could write a book review or a letter to a friend you think might be interested in the book.

4. Did reading the selection give you any ideas for your own writing? You might want to write about:

   • your own fears about death and dying.

   • how the support of a friend, lover or family member helped you through a difficult time.

   • your thoughts or opinions about the AIDS epidemic.

5. If you could talk to Paul Monette, what questions would you ask him about his writing? You might want to write the questions in your journal.

6. You might want to use one or more of the telephone numbers given on pages 58–59 to get more printed information about AIDS and related issues. You could expand your knowledge of the disease and make a presentation to your learning partners.

7. Is there something you kept thinking about after reading the selection from *Borrowed Time*? What? Write about why it is meaningful to you.

About Paul Monette

• ■ •

*P*aul Monette has said in an interview in *Publishers Weekly* that writing *Borrowed Time: An AIDS Memoir* was a form of "mourning and catharsis. I now see that the year I spent writing about Roger after he died . . . was very much a way of staying in the white heat of the fight. Our fight had kept him alive, and since keeping him alive was all I'd wanted to do for two years, doing the writing did the same thing.

"I may have only begun the really bewildering grieving process after I was finished. People ask, 'Was it a hard book to write?' Well, most of it wasn't. It was just so necessary that it didn't matter."

He had another mission as well: "The level of suffering is just not reported [in the press]. The world has not adequately understood the death of a generation of gay men."

In the selection from *Borrowed Time*, Monette speaks about Roger Horwitz's desire to hold on to his work as long as he could before AIDS made working impossible. Then Monette writes, "With him gone, there is just what work I can finish before it overtakes me." Because Monette himself has tested positive for the AIDS virus and because writing is his work, writing has taken on a special importance and urgency for him.

Before 1985 and Roger Horwitz's illness, Paul Monette wrote poetry, screenplays and novels, including *Taking Care of Mrs. Carroll* and *The Long Shot*. Since Roger's death, he has written a volume of poetry called *Love Alone: 18 Elegies for Rog*, as well as two novels, *Afterlife* and *Halfway Home*. His autobiography is *Becoming a Man: Half a Life Story*. Monette has said, "I have seen all the people I love the most struggle to stay alive. That heroism is my reason to stay around. I want to stress the positive in all things I do and say now."

An Update on AIDS

• ■ •

What is AIDS?   Acquired Immune Deficiency Syndrome (AIDS) breaks down the body's immune system, making it unable to fight infection and disease.

What causes AIDS?   AIDS is caused by a virus called HIV, which stands for Human Immunodeficiency Virus. People who have the HIV virus are "HIV positive."

Do all HIV-positive people have AIDS?   No. Even though someone has contracted the HIV virus, it can take years for illness to appear. People infected with HIV may not know they are infected. If illness does develop, it can be mild or very serious. AIDS is the most serious result of HIV infection.

When does HIV infection become AIDS?   A person is diagnosed with AIDS when there is severe damage to the immune system and when he or she has developed one or more of the serious illnesses linked with AIDS. Some people get either tuberculosis or the "AIDS pneumonia," pneumocystis carinii pneumonia (PCP). Others develop Kaposi's sarcoma (KS), a rare form of cancer. Some AIDS patients develop brain disease or spinal cord damage. They may also develop severe bacterial, viral or parasitic infections.

As scientists learn more about AIDS, they are discovering that different groups of people develop different diseases as the result of AIDS. For example, women and IV drug users with AIDS often have cervical cancer and bacterial pneumonia.

Does anyone ever survive AIDS? Some people with AIDS are still alive many years after diagnosis. Early diagnosis and new treatments can help HIV-positive people stay healthy longer. However, since in 1992 there is no cure that will rid the body of the virus, it is not known how long AIDS patients can live.

How is the HIV virus spread from person to person? HIV is spread by direct contact with infected blood or body fluids, including semen, vaginal secretions and breast milk.

What behavior puts a person at risk of HIV infection?

- Unprotected (without a condom) sex—

vaginal, anal or oral—with a person who does not have a clean bill of health.

- Sharing IV drug needles and works.

- HIV-infected women can pass the virus to their children during pregnancy and breastfeeding.

How do you get AIDS from sex? HIV can be spread by sexual intercourse whether you are male or female, heterosexual, bisexual or homosexual. People infected with HIV may have the virus in their semen, vaginal fluid or blood. The virus can enter the other person's body through the membranes of the vagina, rectum or mouth, especially if there are any cuts or sores in those areas or on the penis. The virus cannot be transmitted through the skin, unless the skin is broken or cut and another person's body fluids enter the bloodstream.

Why is IV drug use a high-risk behavior for AIDS? IV drug users often share needles, syringes, cookers and other equipment. Small amounts of blood from an infected person can remain on or in the equipment and be injected into the bloodstream of the next person who uses the equipment.

How can IV drug users protect themselves from AIDS? The best protection is no injection. But if, in spite of all the dangers, you still shoot drugs:

• Never share needles or works.

• If you buy new works on the street, always clean them before using them.

• If you share works, always clean them before you or the next person uses them.

Do condoms help prevent the spread of AIDS? Although they are not 100% effective, condoms are the best preventive measure against AIDS for sexually active people. Condoms should be used according to these guidelines:

1. Use only latex rubber condoms. Lambskin or natural membrane condoms have tiny holes.

2. Use a spermicide (containing nonoxynol-9) in the tip and outside the condom.

3. Use a water-based lubricant (like K-Y jelly or Fore Play) with the condom. Do not use Vaseline, cold cream, baby oil or cooking shortening, which can cause the condom to break.

4. Because condoms can break or come off, it's best for a man to withdraw his penis before coming (ejaculating).

Is HIV transmitted by kissing? Because tiny amounts of HIV have been found in the saliva of some AIDS patients, French kissing or deep kissing may involve some risk. However, casual kissing has not been found to transmit HIV.

Can a person get the HIV virus by being in the same room with an HIV-positive person? People don't get HIV by being around an infected person. The virus is not passed through sneezing, coughing, or drinking from the same glass, or from living in the same house with someone with HIV. HIV is not transmitted through air, food or water, or by touching an object handled, touched or breathed on by an infected person.

However, since toothbrushes and razors can cause cuts and scrapes, it is wise to avoid sharing personal items that may come into contact with the blood of another person.

What is the risk of getting HIV from a blood transfusion? In 1985, blood banks and hospitals began screening blood donors and testing donated blood. Blood that tests positive for HIV is not used for transfusions.

If you had a blood transfusion between the mid-1970s and 1985, and if the source of the transfusion (the hospital or clinic) cannot guarantee that you did not receive infected blood, you may want to take the HIV antibodies test (see next question).

Is there a test for AIDS? A blood test can detect antibodies (substances produced in the blood to fight disease) to HIV. If these antibodies are in the bloodstream, the person has been infected with the virus. However, a positive test for HIV antibodies does not mean a person has AIDS or will develop AIDS.

If you think you have come in contact with the HIV virus, when should you get tested? As soon as possible. The earlier you get tested, diagnosed and treated, the longer you may stay healthy. Anyone being tested should take advantage of the counseling that is available at most testing centers. The counselors have the latest information about HIV and AIDS. They explain the test results and lay out treatment options.

Who should get a test for HIV infection? You should be tested:

- If you have had any sexually transmitted disease.

- If you have shared needles in IV drug use.

- If you are a man and have had sex with another man.

- If you have had sex with a prostitute.

- If you have had sex with anyone who has done any of the things listed above.

- If you are a woman who has been engaging in risky behavior or you plan to have a baby or are not using birth control.

Call the U.S. National AIDS Hotline (1-800-342-2437) for the address of places where you can get counseling and testing.

How is HIV infection treated? New drugs can help control the virus and prevent or delay the symptoms of AIDS. The earlier these drugs are given, the better the chances the HIV-positive person will stay healthy. Some of the new drugs (such as AZT and DDI) attack the virus and help prevent it from growing inside the body. Other drugs treat the cancers and infections that strike HIV-infected people. There are programs to pay for these drugs for patients who can't afford them.

Where to Get
More Information About AIDS
and Treatment Options

• ■ •

U.S. National AIDS Hotline
1-800-342-2437

The hotline is open 24 hours every day to answer questions about HIV infection and AIDS. The people at the hotline can direct callers to counseling and testing centers in their communities.

In Spanish: 1-800-344-7432
(every day, 8 a.m.–2 a.m.)

For the hearing impaired: 1-800-243-7889
(Monday-Friday, 10 a.m.–10 p.m.)

U.S. National AIDS Information Clearinghouse
1-800-458-5231

For printed information on AIDS and HIV infection.

Canadian AIDS Society
1-613-230-3580
(Monday-Friday, 8:30 a.m.–5:30 p.m.)

Provides referrals for community-based treatment agencies in Canada.

AIDS Clearinghouse Canada

1-613-725-3769

Source for education and information.

Gay Men's Health Crisis Hotline (New York City)

1-212-807-6655   (Monday-Friday, 10 a.m.–9 p.m.; Saturday 12 noon–3 p.m.)

This excellent hotline, which takes calls from all across the United States, provides information and counseling on AIDS and safer sex.

National Sexually Transmitted Diseases Hotline

1-800-227-8922   (Monday-Friday, 8 a.m.–11 p.m.)

Offers basic information about sexually transmitted diseases, including free written materials. Provides referrals to local clinics for treatment.

National Institute on Drug Abuse

1-800-662-4357

(Monday-Friday, 9 a.m.–3 a.m.; Saturday-Sunday, 12 noon–3 a.m.)

Gives information and referrals to drug rehabilitation programs.

Use your local telephone directory to find the number of your state or local Health Department. Look in the local and state government sections of the telephone book. Your Health Department can direct you to HIV and AIDS services in your community.

About Keeping a Journal

· ■ ·

*T*he selection from *Borrowed Time: An AIDS Memoir* is a detailed account of both the emotions and the facts that Paul Monette and Roger Horwitz lived with before Roger was diagnosed with AIDS. In the rest of the book, Monette describes the details of their lives during the 19 months Roger was sick, until his death.

Borrowed Time is not written as a journal, but one reason Paul Monette was able to write such a detailed account of his lover's illness and death was that he and Roger both kept journals.

During times of sadness or trouble, keeping a jour nal (sometimes called a diary) can be a way to focus your thoughts. It can help you keep track of important dates and facts. It can also serve as a record of your emotions and of the hopeful and positive things that can happen even in difficult times.

There are no rules about what should and should not go into a journal or diary. While a journal is ideal for keeping track of facts, it is also the place where you can put down thoughts and feelings you do not want to share with anyone. Keeping a journal can be the most private and personal form of writing.

Glossary

• ■ •

The Advocate. A magazine for gay men and
women.

amoebiasis. A disease caused by amoebas, or
intestinal parasites, with symptoms like those of
intestinal flu.

antibodies. Substances produced in the blood
to fight disease organisms.

antivirals. Drugs that prevent the virus that
causes AIDS from multiplying inside the body.

Bactrim. An antibiotic used to treat PCP
(AIDS pneumonia).

blood gas. Blood gases are tested to determine
if a person's vital signs are stable.

bronchoscopy. A medical procedure in which
a flexible instrument is inserted into the
bronchial tube, the main entryway to the lungs.
Also called a "bronc."

CAT scan. An image made by Computerized
Axial Tomography. An x-ray tube surrounds a
specific area of the body and takes pictures of
the internal anatomy from different angles. The
CAT scan allows the diagnosis of diseases of the

brain and spinal cord, cancer and other conditions.

immune dysfunction. The inability of the body to fight off infection and disease.

intestinal flu. A virus disease that causes diarrhea.

IV. Stands for "intravenous," meaning "within the vein"; with an IV unit, patients can be given medicine and nourishment through a needle injected into their veins.

KS (Kaposi's sarcoma). A form of cancer that causes purplish blotches and bumps on the skin.

lymph node. One of a network of glands in the neck, armpit, groin, abdomen and chest that grow large, hard or painful as the body tries to fight off infection or disease.

pneumocystis carinii (PCP). A rare form of pneumonia that frequently strikes AIDS patients.

pulmonary. An adjective referring to the lung.

pulmonary artery. The main blood vessel that carries blood from the heart to the lungs.

simpatico. A Spanish word meaning "likable" or "congenial."

TB (Tuberculosis). A lung disease common among AIDS patients.

T-cell test. T cells are blood cells that fight infection; a lowered T-cell count indicates that the immune system is becoming weak.

thrush. A thick whitish coating on the tongue or in the throat that may be accompanied by a sore throat.

venereal disease. A disease that is transmitted through sex.

walking pneumonia. A mild case of pneumonia.

Three series of good books for all readers:

Writers' Voices—A multicultural, whole-language series of book offering selections from some of America's finest writers, alon with background information, maps, glossaries, questions an activities and many more supplementary materials for readers. Ou list of authors includes: Amy Tan • Alex Haley • Alice Walke • Rudolfo Anaya • Louise Erdrich • Oscar Hijuelos • Maxir Hong Kingston • Gloria Naylor • Anne Tyler • Tom Wolfe Mario Puzo • Avery Corman • Judith Krantz • Larry McMurtr • Mary Higgins Clark • Stephen King • Peter Benchley Ray Bradbury • Sidney Sheldon • Maya Angelou • Jar Goodall • Mark Mathabane • Loretta Lynn • Katherine Jacksc • Carol Burnett • Kareem Abdul-Jabbar • Ted Williams Ahmad Rashad • Abigail Van Buren • Priscilla Presley • Pa Monette • Robert Fulghum • Bill Cosby • Lucille Clifto • Robert Bly • Robert Frost • Nikki Giovanni • Langstc Hughes • Joy Harjo • Edna St. Vincent Millay • Willia Carlos Williams • Terrence McNally • Jules Feiffer • Alfre Uhry • Horton Foote • Marsha Norman • Lynne Alvarez Lonne Elder III • ntozake shange • Neil Simon • Augu Wilson • Harvey Fierstein • Beth Henley • David Mamet Arthur Miller and Spike Lee.

New Writers' Voices—A series of anthologies and individu narratives by talented new writers. Stories, poems and true li experiences written by adult learners cover such topics health, home and family, love, work, facing challenges and li in foreign countries. Many *New Writers' Voices* conta photographs and illustrations.

Reference—A reference library for adult new readers a writers. The first two books in the series are *How to Write Play* and *Discovering Words: The Stories Behind English.*

Write for our free complete catalog:
LVNYC Publishing Program
121 Avenue of the Americas
New York, New York 10013